The Wildlife Art of Ned Smith

The
Wildlife
Art
of
Ned
Smith

Scott Weidensaul

STACKPOLE
BOOKS

Published by
STACKPOLE BOOKS
5067 Ritter Road
Mechanicsburg, PA 17055
www.stackpolebooks.com

Printed in China

10 9 8 7 6 5 4 3 2 1

First edition

On page iii:
DUTCH COUNTRY BLUEBIRDS
acrylic 1984 15 x 22½ inches
COURTESY PENNSYLVANIA GAME COMMISSION

Library of Congress Cataloging-in-Publication Data

Weidensaul, Scott.
    The wildlife art of Ned Smith / Scott Weidensaul.—1st ed.
        p. cm.
    Includes index.
    ISBN 0-8117-0063-1
    1. Smith, Ned, 1919–1985—Catalogs. 2. Wildlife art—Pennsylvania—Catalogs. I.
Smith, Ned, 1919–1985. II. Title.
    N6537.S6168A4 2003
    759.13—dc21
                                                              2003001060

CONTENTS

PILEATED WOODPECKERS
watercolor 1982 12½ x 17½ inches

"Driven by trip-hammer blows, the chisel-like bill of a pileated woodpecker can cut through three inches of solid wood in minutes to uncover and withdraw a borer. The most impressive evidence of this bird's woodworking ability, however, is its nest—a cavity seven inches in diameter and up to two feet deep, chiseled out of the heart of a large forest tree."

—Ned Smith's Wildlife Sketchbook

FOREWORD

E. STANLEY "NED" SMITH WAS A MODEST MAN OF ENORMOUS TALENT. His abilities as an artist, writer, photographer, amateur archaeologist, musician, conservationist, and environmentalist distinguished him, but they never set him apart from the community. Rather, the way in which he married the natural world and the arts connected him forever with humanity—and this is the reason why so many of us are committed to the perpetuation of his ideals. Years after his death, his integrity as a man and an artist comes through clearly in his paintings and his writing.

Ned's commitment to nature and his ability to translate what he saw, heard, and experienced emotionally are national treasures, worth preserving and sharing. That is the mission of the Ned Smith Center for Nature and Art, located in his hometown of Millersburg, Pennsylvania—to bridge the worlds of natural science and creativity. Ten years after Ned's passing, his widow, Marie, gave the center original works worth more than $1.5 million to form the core of our collection. Each year we welcome thousands of visitors to this scenic junction of the Appalachian Mountains and the Susquehanna River. Whether by hiking our trails, strolling our galleries, enjoying a stage performance, or participating in education programs or wildlife research projects, visitors to the Ned Smith Center find themselves enriched by the legacy of this quiet, passionate soul who continues to affect the way we see the world around us. The diversity of the natural world reflects the diversity of our society, and the two are inextricably linked. We remain deeply grateful to Ned Smith for teaching us—and our children and our children's children—how to take delight in that eternal reflection.

Marilyn Derr Kauffman, President
Ned Smith Center for Nature and Art

INTRODUCTION

LIKE MANY PEOPLE, I WAS INTRODUCED TO NED SMITH'S WORK THROUGH the pages of *Pennsylvania Game News*, the monthly magazine of the state's Game Commission. It was the late 1960s, and I was a kid with some small talent for art and a big hunger for anything that had to do with nature. The first time I saw Ned's magazine covers, I was dazzled. Their imagery was so vibrant—the gesture and movement of the animals so fluid and natural, the compositions complex but seemingly effortless, the depiction of the scenes he painted was so *right* that even a youngster like me could recognize it.

About the same time, I used some of my carefully squirreled-away allowance money to buy a copy of *Gone for the Day*, a book based on years of Ned's *Game News* columns—an exploration, month by month, of the natural world in the same Pennsylvania mountains where I lived. The pencil and ink drawings were lovely, but the book captivated me because he described the sorts of fascinating wildlife encounters and unexpected outdoor dramas that kept me roaming the woods. Nor was I alone. *Gone for the Day* has remained in print for more than thirty years on the strength of tens of thousands of naturalists, hunters, anglers, birders, and others who recognize, in its pages, a kindred spirit—someone to whom the outdoors isn't just pretty scenery but an essential part of everyday life, something so close to the core you can't tease it out and call it simply a "hobby."

But for me, the draw was even more significant than that. *Gone for the Day* was a revelation; here was a man with an unapologetic passion and infectious curiosity for nature. It was the first time that I began to suspect it was possible to make a living—and an interesting, exciting one, by the looks of it—from a passion for the outdoors.

I finally met Ned Smith when I was in college, having sent him examples of my own meager efforts at wildlife art. He was generous (probably overly so) in his encouragement, even inviting me to come up to his hometown of Millersburg, in central Pennsylvania,

SPRIGS IN THE WIND
acrylic 1981 16 x 22 inches

where he and his wife, Marie, spent an afternoon talking with me about art, wildlife, and other shared interests. Over the next decade, Ned became something of a mentor, as he had done with many young people trying to break into the ferociously competitive field of nature art. Eventually, I realized my talents lay more in writing than in art, but his work, and his advice, continued to guide me both directly and indirectly as I moved to a freelance career as a natural history writer. In fact, I'm proud to consider Ned's simple, direct style of writing—and especially its unabashed delight at the natural world, which I absorbed as a wide-eyed kid reading and rereading *Gone for the Day*—to be one of the fundamental influences on my own work.

After Ned's unexpected death in 1985 at the age of sixty-five, Marie and I remained in touch, and that friendship strengthened after I and others helped her found the Ned Smith Center for Nature and Art in 1993. She and I had long discussed collaborating on a book showcasing Ned's art, and plans were well under way when a sudden illness robbed us of Marie in January 2002. She is missed, and never more so than by me in assembling this book.

Scott Weidensaul
Schuylkill Haven, PA
November 2002

A LITTLE BIT CAUTIOUS
oil 1984 36 x 24 inches

The Artist

Wildlife, that oldest of human artistic expression whose beginnings are preserved in cave paintings thirty-five thousand years old, has deep roots in North America. While European artists of the eighteenth and nineteenth centuries saw nature as merely a pleasant backdrop, some pioneering artists here, like Mark Catesby and Alexander Wilson, found in the new lands and new species of America great inspiration. Audubon blew the dust off the stuffy Continental approach that had hamstrung his predecessors, infusing the genre with a life and intensity that inspired generations of later masters like Louis Agassiz Fuertes.

The wildlife illustration of Ned Smith stands squarely in this American tradition of the naturalist-artist. Self-taught not only in art but in the natural sciences, Ned nevertheless achieved such a level of expertise that one professor of his acquaintance famously remarked that a walk in the woods with Ned Smith was the equivalent of a college course in field ecology. He brought this remarkable breadth of knowledge to his paintings and drawings, infusing them with a visible understanding of place, season, and subject that few artists have matched.

His professional career spanned more than forty-five years, much of it spent working with state and national wildlife magazines; Ned saw himself not only as an artist, but also as an educator, a commitment that comes through most clearly in his hundreds of articles and columns—he had an unpretentious desire to share that which gave him great pleasure. Because he was able to convey his enthusiasm through a seamless marriage of art, words, and photographs, his efforts were extraordinarily successful, and there are uncounted amateur naturalists who owe their start to his work.

Edmund Stanley Smith—nicknamed "Eddie" when he was small, but later preferring Ned—was born October 19, 1919, in the central Pennsylvania town of Millersburg, which lies on the east shore of the Susquehanna River. It's hard to imagine a more picturesque setting; the Susquehanna at this point is more than a mile wide, flowing through the first of five massive water gaps in the Appalachian ridges that bracket the narrow valleys of this part of Pennsylvania. Long wooded islands dot the river channel, and in summer, low water nearly exposes gravel bars on which grow what the locals call "grass patches": great blooming stands of water-willow, sneezeweed, cardinalflower, and Joe-pye-weed, around which smallmouth bass hide and wait for prey. When Ned was a young man, the river had nesting pairs of bald eagles, and the high cliffs on Mahantongo Mountain just upriver a few miles were a traditional nesting site for peregrine falcons. The ridges were forested and home to deer, wild turkeys, bobcats, and a few black bears. It was, in other words, not only a lovely place for a young artist to grow up, but a nearly perfect habitat for a voraciously inquisitive young naturalist.

Curiosity about the natural world was reinforced in the Smith household to a degree unusual for its day. Mrs. Smith was an avid bird-watcher, while her husband, who managed the local shoe factory, had a particular passion for botany, as well as a talent for writing. Even as a three-year-old, Ned was taken along with them on rambling, walking field trips—the family didn't own a car—through the local hills and farm valleys, and thanks to this early exposure, both Ned and his older brother, Richard, became hooked on nature study. (Richard went on to become a respected amateur botanist, whose books included *Wild Plants of America* and *Wildflowers of the Southern Mountains*. He was also a fair artist in his own right, with a pen-and-ink illustration style resembling that of his brother.)

Ned's aptitude for art showed up early, though it wasn't always appreciated; his first-grade teacher chided him for drawing too much. By age sixteen, his art showed an unusual willingness to tackle complex subjects, though the compositions were often jumbled and the line work awkward. He was, for all practical purposes, self-trained; the small rural high school he attended offered little in the way of art instruction. Although he grew up in the small town, Ned spent his summers working on local farms, and many of his surviving drawings from those days are farm scenes—several men working a thresher, a blacksmith hammering away in his shop, or a horse-drawn sleigh like the one he sometimes drove in winter.

It was on just such a sleigh ride in the winter of 1936, after a now-legendary East Coast blizzard closed the roads for days, that Ned met Marie Reynolds, a vivacious sixteen-year-old who had just transferred in from a one-room schoolhouse out in the country. Marie remembered Ned as a bit of a show-off and, in her words, "a quiet clown" when they were dating in high school, talented not only in art but also in music, playing in the Millersburg Boys' Band and singing in the

THRESHING SCENE
ink 1935 16 x 14 inches

school chorale; in fact, he toyed with the idea of pursuing a career in music before settling on art.

When an aunt who had already paid for Richard's business education made the same offer to Ned he declined, telling her that it would be a waste of his time and her money—but he suggested she instead send him to art school. The aunt, who had lived for a number of years in Switzerland, dismissed the idea out of hand, saying she'd seen too many starving artists in Europe, and so after graduating from high school in 1937, Ned instead went to work for the shoe factory and a tool shop in his hometown.

But he continued to paint. When his sporadic employment at the shoe factory was interrupted by a layoff in May 1938, he packed up his camping gear, food, and some art materials and spent a week in the mountains, sitting all day near a spring with a pair of French binoculars (a gift from the same aunt) and a sketchbook.

"It was a rich, soul-satisfying experience," he wrote almost thirty years later. "Screened by the alders, I was as much a part of the scene as the crumbling stump at my back. All day long songbirds dropped in from the surrounding forest to bathe in the shallow pools and rearrange their feathers in the alders almost within reach. For the first time I saw a yellow, green, and black hooded warbler three feet from my nose. A brilliant scarlet tanager met his reflection in a tiny pool and splashed ecstatically. Ovenbirds, vireos, crested flycatchers, and warblers of every description were hourly visitors . . . One afternoon, a cagey grouse brought her brand-new brood almost to the spring before she saw

E. S. SMITH

Myrtle
Warbler
5/11/39   8.

Black-Throated
Blue Warbler
5/12/39
(see 71+)   9.

10.   Hooded
Warbler
5/12/39
(See 29+)

Phoebe
5/12/39   11.

An early field sketchbook (far left) from 1938 shows warblers Smith painted while camped for a week in the mountains. By the time he painted a pair of northern parulas (left) and two male blackburnian warblers (above) in 1940, he was much better able to capture the pose and gesture of the birds, although his execution was still flat.

me, but when I didn't move she led them away again without fuss or alarm. Deer strolled down a path behind the tent every evening, and as the shadows lengthened the wood thrushes made the mountainside ring with their flutelike song. And the whippoorwills! I fell asleep with their tireless cries whooping in my ears."

Smith himself admitted the watercolor studies he did that week were "amateurish," stiff, and without gesture or spark. But by the next year, his bird paintings had taken on a greater fluidity and animation—still a far cry from the command of draftsmanship he would later exhibit, but nonetheless a remarkable leap from the wooden efforts of the previous year. At the same time, an acquaintance had been bragging about Ned's art to the editor of *Pennsylvania Angler,* the publication of the state Fish Commission, which hired the young man to do a cover painting of bird life along a stream—his first professional assignment.

But Smith's first significant break in illustration came not through wildlife, but because of his interest in firearms. Marie, whom he married in 1945 (insisting they wait until World War II was over), later recalled how many of their dates in high school involved sitting with Ned in his basement shop while he restocked somebody's rifle or shotgun, and he eventually developed a notable skill at the painstaking crafts of engraving metal and checkering wood. That interest, along with Ned's ability with a pencil and brush, prompted a family friend who wrote gun books to recommend him to Samworth Publishing, a major firearms book publisher. His days in the tool shop were over.

At first, Ned's jobs for Samworth mostly entailed drawing guns, cutaways of bullets, and other technical ballistic illustrations—Samworth published textbooks for the FBI, among others—though he also did a variety of trade book jackets on topics like hunting African big game, and firearms of the Civil War and World War I. These were executed before he'd really hit his stride as an artist, and the drawings tend to be a bit flat; the fact that he was often working on subjects with which he had no firsthand experience certainly didn't help. But the association went well enough that in 1947, Thomas G. Samworth, the publisher, invited Ned and Marie to move to his historic Dirleton Plantation, on the Pee Dee River in South Carolina, to work more closely with him and to eliminate the delay of working through the mails.

Samworth, who was also the editor of *American Rifleman* magazine, was something of a character; Marie Smith recalled him in later years as "very dominating—he treated us like kids. He emulated Teddy Roosevelt, running around the plantation all the time in khaki shorts and a white T-shirt, with a shoestring moustache, bare feet, and a pith helmet." He put the Smiths up in the old, rambling house with its balky generator and rats nesting in the bureau drawers, and he clashed with Ned on issues like pay—so that although Marie and Ned enjoyed South Carolina, and might have stayed under different circumstances, after several months they returned home to Pennsylvania. Ned continued to work for Samworth for another two years, occasionally commuting to South Carolina, before finally quitting to take a job with the Pennsylvania Game Commission.

There is, perhaps, no better way to trace the growth and maturity of Ned Smith's artwork than in the pages of *Pennsylvania Game News,* the agency's small but widely read magazine. From his first employment in the late 1940s, through his years as staff illustrator in the '50s and '60s, and in later years as a freelance artist, he painted nearly 120 *Game News* covers and created thousands of pencil or ink illustrations for its articles.

Many of the early cover paintings were somewhat labored attempts at humor common in sporting magazines of the day, usually repeating a variant of the "thwarted hunter" theme—a deer hunter hiding behind a tree and scowling at a loud-mouthed jay that has alerted a large buck to his presence; a turkey that is sneaking through the brush around an unsuspecting hunter; another hapless fellow who, with a sandwich jammed in his mouth and both hands full while pouring a sloshing cup of coffee, looks up to see a black bear about to bolt from sight.

By the 1960s, however, readers were seeing more of what would become Ned's strength and signature—realistic wildlife portraiture. A bull elk stands beneath soft green hemlocks in a snowy northern Pennsylvania forest; a cottontail explodes from a thicket beneath the noses of two beagles. The power of his paintings lay not in their detail—there are many other artists who slavishly render every feather and hair with far less successful results—but rather the ability Ned had to capture the essence of the bird or mammal or fish, to let the fundamental character of the species shine through.

There is a cheekiness to his red squirrels, a playfulness to his river otters, and an arrogance to his white-tailed buck that come through observation and field sketching. He knew wildlife because he watched the real thing, studied it, drew it from life on an almost daily basis. He was obsessive about getting outside as much as possible, unlike many artists who work primarily from captive specimens or photographs. (Ned recognized the value of photographic reference, too, eventually accumulating tens of thousands of color transparencies that documented the minutiae of the natural world, but the core of his work was field sketching and close observation, not copying from photos.) Because of his command of the environment he was portraying, not even his backgrounds are generic; a glance at the distant woods behind one of his deer tells the experienced eye that the trees that grow there are white oak and hemlock, or that the shrubs out of which a pair of woodcock are rising are speckled alder that have gone to seed. There is an inherent authenticity to his work that is instantly apparent to anyone who knows wildlife—and the *Game News* audience, which knew wildlife very well, embraced the young man's work.

PENNSYLVANIA LONG RIFLE
AND ACCOUTERMENTS
ink 1976 4 x 6½ inches

The Pennsylvania long rifle—one of the enduring symbols of the Eastern frontier, and an extraordinary blend of artistry and functionality—fascinated Smith, who drew the firearm frequently over the years. These two small ink works show a unique double-barreled long rifle with its accessories and a selection of the brass inlays and stock carvings found on later rifles.

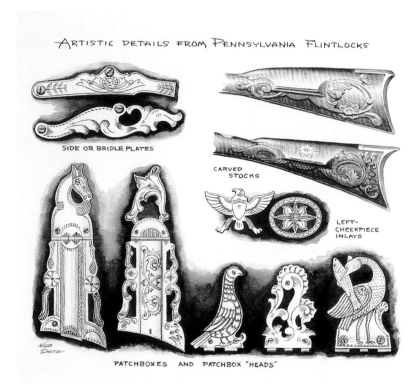

LONG RIFLE PATCHBOXES
ink wash undated 10 x 9 inches

Two early Pennsylvania Game News *covers show the "thwarted hunter" theme common in sporting illustration, which Smith's editors often had him return to.* COURTESY PENNSYLVANIA GAME COMMISSION

"I know it's trite to say that the wildlife artist should try to impart the essence of the creature and its surroundings," he said in later years. "I'm sure we all try for that. But I'm not happy unless I get the feeling that I've been there when I'm painting. If that feeling doesn't come over me at some point, then something is wrong."

Even good artists make mistakes, of course, especially when deadlines are bearing down. One assignment Ned received was to redo a series of bird and mammal posters that were originally painted by the noted illustrator Jacob Bates Abbott in the 1940s. Ned did eight large paintings—mammals of the mountains, mammals of fields and woodlots, waterfowl, raptors, and so on—and completed the last one, showing two dozen forest songbirds, by pulling an all-nighter at the easel. It wasn't until almost twenty years later, after the posters had been through uncounted printings, that someone

pointed out that in his tired haste, the artist had forgotten to give a scarlet tanager its pair of legs. One problem with popularity is that your mistakes, as well as your successes, stick around for a long time; that legless tanager and all the rest of the posters are still in print.

Although he dabbled in oils as a young artist, the medium isn't well suited to illustration because of its long drying time, and so much of Smith's early color work was done in transparent watercolor. By the 1960s, though, he'd begun to shift to acrylic paint, first using the new medium in the opaque drybrush style in vogue with illustrators, or in thin washes, as though it were watercolor. Later he fused acrylic's dual transparency and opacity while making best use of its vivid colors (which added punch otherwise lost in reproduction) and its quick drying time, which saved hours on tight deadlines.

YELLOW-BREASTED CHAT

pencil and white tempera 1968 8½ x 13 inches

The cover paintings for *Game News* were occasional assignments, but each month's issue featured a dozen or more pencil, ink, or wash illustrations, ranging from elaborate double-page compositions to thumbnail cartoons. As his painting had made rapid strides, his black-and-white art developed as well. By the early 1960s, Ned had settled comfortably into a flexible mixed-media style well suited to both his temperament and the demands of magazine reproduction—often using a gray-toned illustration board as a neutral background, then working up and down the value scale with pencil, ink washes, and highlights of white tempera, either delicately or as a thicker opaque. The technique offered the best of both worlds—the softness and flexibility of pencil with the sparkle and crispness of tempera.

Ned's other favorite medium—and one at which he was an acknowledged master—was pen and ink. Line art is extraordinarily deceptive. The viewer sees a minimalistic rendering and may be tempted to refer to it as a "sketch," implying that it is half-finished or rough. Nothing could be farther from the truth. The process of paring down the image—stripping away the superfluous, finding the visual core and expressing it with relatively few lines—is one of the hardest tasks in all of art, and few media are as demanding of an artist than a bottle of ink and a sharp steel nib.

Line direction, control, and intensity are integral to ink drawing, and in these Ned Smith was unmatched. The flowing lines convey the grain of dead wood, the overlap of feathers, or the way the shadow of a sassafras sapling lies across the snow—and in turn, it shows the humps and hummocks of the ground *beneath* the snow as well. Knowing what to add is important, but even

COPPERHEAD
ink 1968 3½ x 3½ inches

more crucial is understanding what to leave out—how to show the glossy coat of a black bear through an abundance of white space, for example.

Game News was a tutorial for the young artist not only in deadline art, but the whole world of magazine publishing. In 1951, he was promoted to acting editor when his boss was called up to active military service in Korea, and for the next two years he juggled editing along with a somewhat reduced art load. Once the war was over, Ned branched out, leaving his staff artist position in 1953 to become a full-time freelancer, a career he would keep for the rest of his life. While he always maintained a close association with the Pennsylvania

LEFT: *Chats are a declining species in much of the East, where they inhabit brushy thickets, blackberry tangles, and old, overgrown fields. Created for "Gone for the Day," this drawing is typical of Smith's pencil illustration, using the toned board as a neutral background, then working down the value scale with pencil while adding white highlights with paint.*

"June 2—*For all his brilliant beauty the yellow-breasted chat is somewhat of a clown. He delights in keeping out of sight, slipping through his tangled haunts like a shadow. When he does cross from one thicket to another he does so with a tantalizing, but awkward, flourish, his tail flopping loosely as though attached by a string.*

Not only is he a clever mimic, but his song has an uncanny ventriloquial quality. This afternoon I was sitting on a sunny hillside when a chat mounted a blackberry cane less than twenty feet away and began to sing. His repertoire consisted of only three different notes tirelessly repeated in the same sequence. All were borrowed from other birds—the alarm note of the robin, the house sparrow's chip, and the caw of the crow. The quality of each was perfect, but the crow's caw was the most amazing. So cleverly was it muted that I listened for some time before I realized that it came from the chat, and not a crow half a mile across the valley." —Gone for the Day

WALKIN' SHOES
By NED SMITH

The Mallard—Cosmopolitan Dandy

1. Mallards are poor table birds. True or false?
2. Are mallards classed as puddle ducks or diving ducks?
3. What is a duck's speculum?
4. Do mallards spend the winter in Pennsylvania?
5. Wild mallards sometimes attain a weight of five pounds. True or false?
6. Do mallards eat acorns?
7. Mallards run across the surface of the water before taking off. True or false?
8. Is it true that some ducks can't fly during part of the summer?
(Answers on Page 60)

JUST above the shore line treetops a pair of wild ducks coursed out over the river, racing ahead of the wind with shallow, but powerful wingbeats. Nothing about the female invited a second look, but even against the stormy sky the drake's ashen plumage, contrasting sharply with a dark green head and mahogany chest, marked him as a mallard.

They skipped a few wingbeats as a tree-studded island passed beneath them, then turned and made a wide sweep over the far shore. Circling, they returned, made a tighter pass around the island, and let down the flaps over a quiet eddy on the downstream side.

The river was the Susquehanna in Pennsylvania. It could as easily have been a stream in France, or perhaps in Iceland, or North Africa, or China, or Korea, for "our" beloved mallard makes his home in practically all of the Northern Hemisphere below the Arctic Circle.

In perfect plumage a wild mallard drake is a handsome bird, crowned by an iridescent green head and neck that glow with blue and violet highlights in the sunshine. His haughty chest is a rich purplish chestnut, set off from the neck by an immaculate white collar.

The body plumage is chiefly gray-pale and finely vermiculated on the underparts, brownish above. The tail is whitish; the black central upper tail coverts are curiously curled.

The wings are chiefly gray-brown except for the speculum, a rich, iridescent blue patch bordered in front and behind by a band of black, then a band of white.

The bill is yellow with a black nail; the feet and legs are orange or vermillion.

The hen is a nondescript mottled buff and gray-brown, considerably darker above. Her bill is dull orange with dusky spotting. Her wings are similar to the drake's, but duller.

Wild mallards are smaller and more streamlined than their domestic counterparts, the drakes averaging a shade less than three pounds. Domestic birds, on the other hand, frequently weigh a pound or two more.

OCTOBER, 1964   3

Smith's "Walkin' Shoes" column ran from 1958 through 1965 in Game News. COURTESY PENNSYLVANIA GAME COMMISSION

Game Commission, he was soon supplementing *Game News* assignments with work for national publications like *Field & Stream*.

His shift to freelancing also gave Ned an opportunity to write much more. Although his reputation is grounded on his art, Smith was from the beginning an equally adept writer, and throughout his career he combined art and writing to great effect, especially in a series of magazine columns stretching almost unbroken for more than twenty-five years. He wasn't given to lyricism or verbal flourishes—his style was conversational and unembroidered, always clear, often with a leavening dose of humor, much of it gently self-deprecating. "Twenty-five years is a long time, but I remember that gray December day as though it were yesterday," he wrote in an installment of "Walkin' Shoes," a column that ran in *Game News* from 1958 through 1965:

I was hurrying back to my new job at the tool factory by a shortcut that led down a crooked path, across a footbridge, and up a weedy hillside on the edge of town. Just over the bridge a bird whirred up from the ground and perched on a bobbing wild sunflower stalk at my elbow. It was a strange and colorful bird, and as I stared a staccato chorus of loud calls revealed more of them sitting on neighboring weedstalks.

They were evening grosbeaks. I recognized them at once from the picture in my well-thumbed Chester Reed's "Bird Guide," but in the flesh they were infinitely more beautiful than the bird in that dingy illustration. Late for work? I'm afraid I was.

LADIES' MAN
acrylic 1980 18 x 26 inches

16

RED FOX
acrylic 1965 9½ x 15 inches

An unusual monochromatic acrylic, this red fox was the main illustration for the first installment of "Gone for the Day" when the column debuted in Game News in January 1966.

In another "Walkin' Shoes" column, he describes a flock of tundra swans coming in for a landing:

> Occasionally a flock would come in high, mere backlighted specks in the sky, and spiral slowly overhead. Then setting their wings into a stiff bow and holding their heads aloft on gracefully arched necks, they would give themselves to the invisible updrafts and hang suspended in the blue. Their balance was perfect. From below you could detect no movement—they just hung there like paper cutouts.
>
> Then almost imperceptibly they settled earthward, still unmoving, but gradually growing larger and larger, until at last they settled upon the water like thistledown. The effect was so unreal I almost wondered if I had really seen it at all.

"Walkin' Shoes" was popular with readers, but in 1966 he decided to try something different—an illustrated column based on his extensive field journals and crafted as an informal diary of his outdoor wanderings. Called "Gone for the Day," the columns proved to be far more popular than Ned or his *Game News* editors could have imagined, and in 1971, a few years after their four-year run was concluded, the Game Commission published them in book form. That book remains in print more than three decades later, an acknowledged classic of Pennsylvania nature writing.

"As is true of anyone who bums around the woods, my sylvan snooping has led to innumerable interesting discoveries—a rare bird here, an unusual flower there; an exciting incident in the life of a wild animal, or a strange insect performance—all sorts of happenings," he wrote in the introduction to the first column. "Being a confirmed writer-downer, I have accumulated reams of notes, stacks of sketches, and a shameful number of color photographs. But not only have these notes and pictures been of inestimable value to me as a wildlife artist and nature writer, they have also recalled with poignant pleasure many of the nearly forgotten incidents that make nature snooping so much fun."

He also noted in that inaugural column that reading about someone else's experiences can be "as painfully boring as someone else's family album," but he was counting on nature's inherent ability to captivate any audience. That certainly proved to be the case with

COTTONTAIL
ink 1979 9¾ x 7¾ inches

"Gone for the Day," but Smith used a careful eye and ear in selecting only the most interesting anecdotes from his decades' worth of journals, then editing them down to a tight, entertaining nugget.

> *August 14*—The banks along our mountain roads are flecked with the squatty, snow-white mushrooms known as peppery lactarius. Years ago I learned the appropriateness of its name by touching my tongue to a drop of the milky juice that oozes from breaks in its gills. Today a friend insisted on learning the same way and lapped up a big drop of the fiery stuff. There was a slight delay—attributable to reaction time, I suppose. Then an incredulous look flashed across his face, followed by a fit of the most inspired and copious expectorating you can imagine. A fervent "Wow" was his only comment, but it spoke volumes.

Ned used his column as a bully pulpit to push several themes that were of lasting importance to him—calling attention to less-appreciated aspects of the natural world, like insects and small vertebrates, or extolling the virtues of gathering native foods like mushrooms, berries, and nuts; not surprisingly, the wild-foods guru Euell Gibbons, author of *Stalking the Wild Asparagus* and other books, was a friend of Ned and Marie's.

Ned's columns could sometimes carry a whiff of smugness, too, especially on the subject of modern America's infatuation with speed and convenience. "Sunday afternoon traffic dotted both routes with steady streams of antlike autos," he wrote about sitting on a lonely ridge above the Susquehanna, "and I could imagine the weariness and frustration that were being spawned in that distant manifestation of progress and civilization. 'Pleasure driving,' some call it, but watching from high on a hill under April's broad blue sky I didn't feel I was missing a thing."

Some of the best writing in "Gone for the Day," however, simply gave the reader a strong sense of place and season.

September 28—The river is a great place to watch the arrival of autumn, even on a rainy day. I let my canoe hang up on a ledge above Half-Falls Island along about sunset, and, with my bugging rod idly lying across athwart, just sat there and took it in. It was a colorless scene. Water and sky were veiled by a gray mixture of drizzle and mist. The "grass patches," the drying sedges on the islands, and the willows themselves, were a fading, nondescript olive-and-ochre. The only real color in sight was a patch of bright yellow sneezeweed on a nearby sandy island. But there was a melancholy beauty about the somber scene that seemed entirely in keeping with the passing of summer.

For a time there was only the sound of rippling water and the clamor of grackles on a distant island. Then I heard a melodious yodelling cry, and a small flock of yellowlegs materialized out of the mist, speeding downriver on pointed wings. They passed by with a rush, but soon turned and came back to alight on a gravel bar, where they ran about on slender legs, feeding hurriedly in the little daylight that remained.

In the morning they will be gone, heading for the coast, then south to their wintering grounds. Where will they stop? Who knows? Maybe Florida or Cuba or South America. Wherever their ancestors before them waited out the winter, there they will call a halt.

The raw materials for "Gone for the Day" were Smith's voluminous field journals; he spent at least part of almost every day outside, regardless of the season, and even when work kept him penned up in his basement studio, he had half an eye cocked out the sliding glass doors near his drawing table, watching the animals that came to the yard he and Marie had landscaped specifically for wildlife.

Ned wasn't kidding when he told his readers he was a "confirmed writer-downer"—he eventually compiled nearly forty years' worth of meticulous journals, cataloged in a long shelf's worth of three-ring-binder notebooks, to say nothing of uncounted field sketches and pencil or watercolor studies. Journaling was a daily habit, with Smith jotting notes and doing quick sketches in the field, then writing them out in longhand
(text continues on page 22)

GREATER YELLOWLEGS
watercolor 1978 13 x 20 inches

At a time when he had switched largely to acrylic for his magazine covers, Smith instead chose to do this painting of a greater yellowlegs in transparent watercolor, a choice that brings out the soft, humid feel of an overcast summer day and works well with the muted colors of both the bird and its surroundings.

BLACK-CROWNED NIGHT HERON
ink 1968 3½ x 3½ inches

SPUR OF THE MOMENT
watercolor 1970 26 x 18 inches

WINTER CARDINALS
acrylic 1985 11 x 14 inches

*One of Smith's final works,
this painting incorporates an
unusual design element, the
cuplike seedheads of tulip trees
catching the fresh snow, which
lend an almost Oriental feel
to the composition.*

SHOWY LADY'S-SLIPPER
watercolor and pencil undated 5½ x 7 inches

RUFFED GROUSE
watercolor undated 12 x 12 inches

later in the day when he was at home. Then Marie would type them up, with Ned adding any explanatory drawings.

The diary entries readers found in "Gone for the Day" were tightly edited, but the journals from which they were drawn show a much more eclectic range of interests, including some, like mycology, that only rarely appeared in the columns (perhaps because Smith realized most hunters and naturalists didn't share his passion for fungi).

Many days, the journals were simply annotated lists of what he'd seen while hiking—what wildflowers were in bloom, which berries were ripe and where the heaviest concentrations were, what insects he turned up in a thorough search of a goldenrod clump. Taken together, they provide an unmatched daily snapshot of the changing seasons in the central Appalachians over the course of four decades. Very little escaped his notice. A grouse hunt with a friend in November 1964 resulted in bagging three birds—and a list, in that evening's notes, of what the crops of the grouse contained:

19 acorns (prob. bl[ack] oak)
12 unid. buds
4 witch hazel flowers
3 blueberry buds
62 pieces of wintergreen leaves (many sm. ones)

---

2 laurel buds
7 acorns
174 witch hazel flowers (sans petals)
11 witch hazel buds
2 wintergreen berries
15 pieces of wintergreen leaves (equiv. of 6 leaves)
2 laurel seed capsules
7 blueberry buds
3 unid. buds
1 spider

---

7 acorns
3 wintergreen berries
2 pieces wintergreen leaf (1 leaf)
126 witch hazel flowers (most with petals)

Large numbers of acorns & witch hazel flowers are unusual. <u>Many</u> small acorns on trees & ground this fall—esp. bl. and scarlet oak. Few scrub oak. Very few greenbrier berries except on high ground. Almost no wintergreen berries.

Another grouse shot along Wolf Pond Rd. 11/2 contained:

1 chestnut oak acorn
10 black oak acorns
2 pieces laurel leaf
7 pieces greenbrier leaf
1 unid. bud
4 pieces grit

A few days later, while walking out of the woods from another grouse-hunting trip—Smith was a passionate grouse hunter every autumn—he encountered a pair of great horned owls.

After unloading my gun at quitting time . . . I hooted 2 or 3 times in an attempt to imitate the one with the deeper voice & soon saw him (or her) heading my way. Approaching, he set his wings & glided with them stretched straight out like an eagle's to the top of a tall tree only about 50 ft. from where I stood. I squeaked, but he merely looked down at me. It was surprising that he didn't recognize me as a human, for the light was good; in fact, the setting sun still struck him at the top of the tree, and I was wearing a <u>brilliant</u> fire-orange fluorescent hunting cap. I hooted several times before he replied, raising his tail nearly to the vertical as he hooted. The wind buffeted his "horns" & made his perch in the small branches precarious. Each time I hooted he answered, then suddenly he "turned down the volume." Every hoot thereafter was so soft I doubt the last notes could have been heard at any distance. I answered in like fashion. His song was like this:

Sometimes a seventh note was added at the end. The other owl's hoot was pitched much higher, much like a barred owl. A gray squirrel nearby objected to our hooting and scolded continuously. When he barked excitedly the owl swiveled his head around & looked his way, but stayed put. . . . As he departed I hooted, [and] he answered as he flew. The other owl immediately began hooting, and as I walked out along the ridge I could hear them conversing in the light of the rising full moon.

To an artist with such an abiding drive to get every detail right, sweating the small stuff mattered. The late outdoor writer Jim Bashline, who was Smith's longtime friend and a former editor of his at *Game News*, once

FIELD SKETCHES
pencil and watercolor 1982
Swamp Sparrow:
    11 x 7¾ inches
Puttyroot Orchid:
    8 x 11 inches

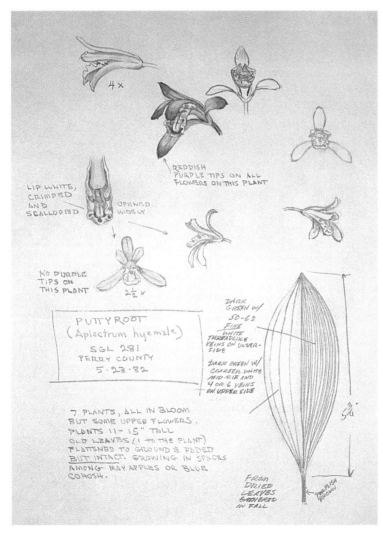

These two field sketches, made late in Ned Smith's life, are typical of the meticulous attention to details—both form and color—that he tried to record in his field notes and drawings. Birds and mammals were usually drawn from life, by watching through a spotting scope. The marten, below, was a studio drawing.

MARTEN
ink undated 7 x 9 inches

recalled taking Ned on his first salmon-fishing trip to New Brunswick in the 1960s. Camped with a group on the Little Southwest Miramichi, fishing without a guide in a pool that wasn't supposed to hold any fish, Ned managed to land a twelve-pound Atlantic salmon, the best fish out of the river that month:

> Others in camp were shocked but happy and much back-slapping and huzzaing took place. Smith acknowledged the cheers but he immediately went to work with his camera photographing the fish from all angles, taking numerous close-ups of insignificant details. Before we went to sleep that night the last thing I remember him saying was, "Say, did you notice that the maxillary bone on that fish did not extend as far to the rear as it does on most other salmon? You know, I've never seen that pointed out in reference books before."

Fish bones weren't all he was interested in; Ned applied the same attention to subjects as diverse as prehistoric archaeology and the unique style of duck-hunting boat found on the Susquehanna. He had a knack for tinkering and invention, and his early days as a metal lathe operator left him with the skills to convert his ideas into reality—creating a nifty folding tripod made of aluminum strapping that fit easily into a pack, or crafting a better safety for his favorite .300 Savage deer rifle (a design better suited to a left-handed shooter like Ned, and one the gun maker itself finally adopted decades later).

Although the vast majority of Ned's illustration work was for magazines, he also was tapped regularly by authors and publishers to illustrate books. Unlike his early work with Samworth, these assignments gave him a chance to play to his strengths. One early commission was to illustrate *The Complete Book of the Wild Turkey,* by his friend and colleague Dr. Roger Latham. In 1971, he created a series of lovely pencil drawings for *Iron-tail,* a book tracing the life of an Everglades alligator, and a few years later he illustrated Hal H. Harrison's *Field Guide to Bird Nests,* part of the legendary Peterson field guide series. In 1981, he illustrated the two-volume

RIVER OTTERS
acrylic 1983 15 x 22½ inches COURTESY PENNSYLVANIA GAME COMMISSION

Book of Mammals by the National Geographic Society. He also did the line art for *Ecology and Field Biology,* first published in 1966, which remains the standard college textbook on the subject; now in its sixth edition, it retains many of Ned's complex and elegant drawings, such as a cross-section through a beach and tidal zone, showing the various invertebrates living there.

Throughout his life, Ned Smith had his strongest following in the East, but as his book illustrations show, he enjoyed a national audience as well from his early years. He was a regular contributor to *Sports Afield* and *Field & Stream* magazines, doing cover and interior illustrations; the latter magazine also produced a popular print series based on a portfolio of his gamebird paintings, which debuted at a private reception in the

American Museum of Natural History in New York. Ned also drew and wrote the long-running "Sportsman's Quiz" column in *Sports Afield*, a monthly puzzler that mixed natural history and fishing and hunting trivia with his line drawings. Over the years, his art and writing appeared in more than three dozen magazines around the U.S., but beginning in 1965 he acquired an especially wide readership through a new column, "Wildlife Sketchbook," which he did for *National Wildlife* magazine.

Working most often in ink, he produced one- or two-page columns on topics that allowed him to show off his exceptional skills with a pen—one on winter tracking, for instance, deciphered the clues in intersecting lines of prints through snowy fields, ending with a red fox lunging at a flushing pheasant; others detailed the bird life along a wintry beach, or showed a pack of wolves pulling down a cow moose. The large format gave him a lot of freedom to try complex compositions that were near the pinnacle of his abilities in

COMMON YELLOWTHROAT AND
LOUISIANA WATERTHRUSH
ink undated 4¼ x 8 inches

LOOKING FOR TROUBLE (with preliminary sketches)
acrylic 1981 15 x 21 inches

Working on a variety of thumbnails for a painting of an elk in a western setting, Smith settled on one, then blocked it out in order to scale up the drawing to its full size.

SPORTSMAN'S QUIZ
By NED SMITH

1.

A white-tailed buck can run faster than 35 mph.

☐ True   ☐ False

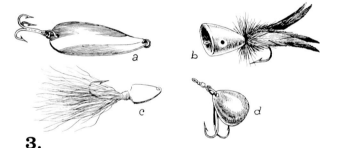

3.

Can you match these lures with the fish they catch?

☐ Rainbow trout   ☐ Bonefish   ☐ Pike

☐ Largemouth bass

5.

Wood ducks nest in tree cavities, and the young leave the nest soon after hatching. How do the young reach the ground or water?

. . . .

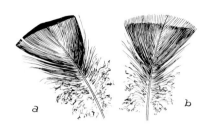

2.

Which breast feather is from a wild turkey

☐ Gobbler   ☐ Hen

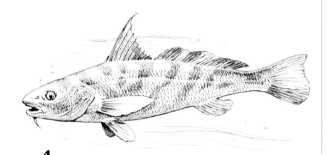

4.

The whiting, or kingfish, is often caught in shallow water along the beaches.

☐ True   ☐ False

the WHATIZZIT corner

6.

This small nut is enjoyed by people and wildlife. What is it?

. . . .

One popular feature that ran for years in Sports Afield *during the '60s and '70s was Ned Smith's monthly "Sportsman's Quiz." Combining line art with outdoor brainteasers, it also gave him an opportunity to bring a lot of natural history information into the magazine, but he eventually dropped the column when it became too time-consuming—not drawing the artwork, but researching back through more than a hundred previous installments to see if a particular question or puzzle had been used before.*

COURTESY SPORTS AFIELD

the medium. He wrote and illustrated the column on a regular basis for thirteen years, and in 1988 the magazine's publisher, the National Wildlife Federation, released a compilation book under the title *Ned Smith's Wildlife Sketchbook.*

Smith saw himself as a working freelancer, with few illusions about what that meant in terms of his art and its impact; he often joked that he'd like to see everything he ever illustrated in one huge pile—though he thought the sight of such a huge, tottering mound would slightly depress him. But he clearly also saw himself as an emissary and educator on behalf of the natural world. In an unpublished notebook entry that was to have been the basis of a later article, Smith wrote about what he called "the soft sell" of wildlife art in reaching audiences hungry for information about nature.

Unlike the written word, paintings can't quote statistics or explain complex theories. They are limited to whatever statements can be made with paint and pencil. But, over the years, this has been quietly and steadily effective.

The soft sell involves painting realistically and without sensationalism. The artist's grouse should look haughty, his mice should look timid, and his elk should bounce when they walk. He should include a slice of habitat to show that woodcock need damp cover and pronghorns need space. Some paintings might show typical food plants, or the interaction with other species. His wild animals should look wild and alert, not the dense, overweight pets that play their roles on television.

In short, the soft sell consists of portraying the animal or bird realistically and honestly. That's all the artist can do. If he's successful, the viewer will learn a great deal about wildlife, but, more than that, will be inspired to get out-of-doors and look for himself.

This passage is telling, because it reveals a great deal about Ned Smith's approach to art in general, and explains both the strengths and weaknesses of his art.

The strengths are self-evident—the almost uncanny way he had of conjuring up the essence of a wild animal and placing it in the heart of its world. One

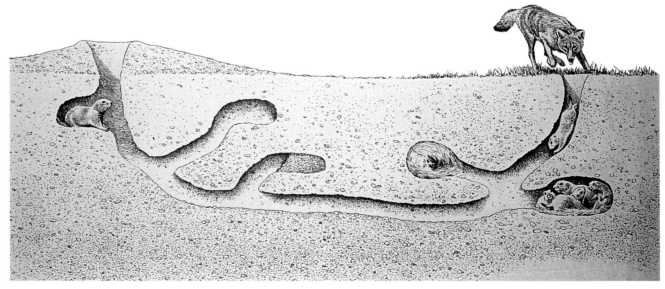

PRAIRIE DOG BURROW

ink 1981 16 x 8 inches COURTESY NATIONAL GEOGRAPHIC SOCIETY

THE PURSUIT
acrylic undated 22 x 15 inches

One of a series of illustrations for the book Iron-tail *by George X. Sand, about the life of an alligator in the Florida Everglades.*

FIGHTING ALLIGATORS
pencil 1971 15 x 20 inches

could argue, however, that his paintings and drawings are too literal, too accurate and complete; that in faithfully rendering the natural world he saw, he left out an essential part of himself. This is a charge that is often leveled against wildlife art as a genre, not only Ned Smith's work—but it's a criticism most often made by those to whom the natural world is irrelevant. For a naturalist-artist, wild animals and wild places *are* an essential part of the internal landscape, as real and vital as any human emotion that might be expressed on canvas or paper.

Ned Smith made no particular bones about being an illustrator, which for him was as much an occasion to explain and educate as it was an artistic opportunity; even in later years, when he was painting oils for the limited-edition market, there was a fundamental honesty about his paintings that resonates with the people who most intimately know the subjects and the land he depicted. And they, perhaps, are the best and final judges.

Certainly, during his lifetime Smith achieved both popular and professional acclaim, which, like his work, encompassed artistic and educational importance. He was the recipient of the Baltimore Art Director's Gold Medal Award, for instance, and his painting of a gyrfalcon was chosen to accompany a world tour of bird art by the prestigious Leigh Yawkey Woodson Art Museum—but he was also honored by the American Association for Conservation Education.

The rise of the environmental movement in the 1970s, coupled with a greater awareness of the natural world and growing numbers of people with an interest in wildlife, fueled the once-small market for signed limited-edition nature art prints, which expanded beyond the handful of winners of the annual federal duck stamp contest. In 1978, Ned entered this market with the first of three self-published works, "The Goshawk's Tribute," which depicted an adult goshawk with a blue jay; this was followed by "Spring Gobbler" and "Big Red," the latter a painting of a red fox pausing at the crest of a snowdrift, which became one of the most popular prints he ever released. Yet marketing and shipping the prints proved to be an enormous hassle for the artist—one room of Ned and Marie's house was stacked full of mailing boxes—and beginning in 1980, his subsequent prints were published by Sportsman Specialties of Youngwood, Pennsylvania.

Some of the paintings, like "Windfall Grouse" and "December Snow," first appeared on *Game News*, but focusing on the booming print market gave Ned greater freedom to work on large easel paintings instead of remaining within the narrower confines of illustration

WHITE-TAILED PTARMIGAN IN AUTUMN.

NED SMITH-

BELOW-PTARMIGAN IN WINTER.

LEFT- IT'S HARD TO BELIEVE BOTH THESE BIRDS ARE BLACK-BELLIED PLOVERS. ONE APPEARS IN HIS PALE WINTER PLUMAGE; THE OTHER IN HIS BOLDLY MARKED SPRING DRESS.

Ptarmigan, plovers, and the eroding tips of a house sparrow's feather all show how bird plumages change with the seasons.

PLUMAGES
ink undated 15 ½ x 7 ¼ inches

SETTER
watercolor undated 14½ x 10¼ inches

As a naturalist, Ned had a realistic view of the harsh realities of
predation, but as an artist, he was somewhat constrained in how
much of that reality his audience was willing to see. This large pen
drawing, done for a "Wildlife Sketchbook" column, is an exception.

"Avoiding the lashing hooves, some of the wolves will tear at
the running animal's flanks and rump . . . Another wolf usually
races ahead and fastens its teeth into the moose's throat or, more
often, its bulbous nose . . . The moose's size usually precludes a
quick kill. Instead, the moose must be relentlessly harassed, torn,
and weighed down until the cumulative effect is death, probably
due to a combination of loss of blood, exhaustion, and shock."

MOOSE AND WOLVES
ink undated

COURTESY NATIONAL WILDLIFE FEDERATION

assignments, and to enjoy the chance to work with oils instead of the acrylics he'd so long favored; the slower medium gave his later works a depth that the acrylics couldn't match. He also felt freer to explore subjects with a wider geographic reach than most of his work had shown—a pair of moose in a Canadian bog, for instance, or a pack of gray wolves racing through a North Woods snowstorm.

By the early 1980s, Ned Smith's national reputation made him a popular choice for art-based fund-raisers, both by state agencies and private organizations. In 1983, he was given the honor of creating Pennsylvania's "first of state" waterfowl stamp design, which showed a pair of wood ducks in flight among old sycamores. Two years later, he was invited again to paint the state stamp design; this time he chose a pair of mallards leaping out of a marsh. Duck stamp art has, over the decades, become highly formulaic and rigid in

STING OF THE HOOK
acrylic 1981 14 x 17 inches

its conventions, and generally stiff and overdone in its execution. Ned's two works, by contrast, show what the genre can be when a master infuses it with fresh life.

Likewise, he accepted a number of commissions to help conservation groups whose goals he supported, like the National Wild Turkey Federation and Hawk Mountain Sanctuary in Pennsylvania. Smith had been visiting Hawk Mountain for decades and he marked the world famous sanctuary's fiftieth anniversary by donating a large oil he had painted especially for the occasion, "Hawk Mountain Gold," showing two golden eagles soaring past the ridge-top lookout—though he grumbled a bit when the painting was returned with a request to "make it a bit more gold" by punching up the yellows in the autumnal background. He complied, but the request rankled, if only because he knew the oak-covered Pennsylvania hills never look that lemony.

BIG WOODS BOBCAT
acrylic 1984 15 x 22½ inches

This was the third and last of a series of prints Smith was commissioned to paint for the Pennsylvania Game Commission to raise money for nongame wildlife conservation; "Big Woods Bobcat" was released just before his death.

COURTESY PENNSYLVANIA GAME COMMISSION

SYCAMORE CREEK WOODIES
acrylic 1983 16¾ x 12½ inches

This painting, commissioned in 1983, was Pennsylvania's "first of state" duck stamp design, a rare honor for any wildlife artist.

COURTESY PENNSYLVANIA GAME COMMISSION

His involvement also jump-started the Pennsylvania Game Commission's "Working Together for Wildlife" print series, which raises money specifically for non-game wildlife conservation. His subjects over the course of three years were a couple of playful river otters, a resting bobcat, and a family of eastern bluebirds nesting in a wooden fencepost, in front of a classic Pennsylvania German barn. "Dutch Country Bluebirds" is a beautiful, appealing work, and has proven to be one of the most enduringly popular of Ned's prints; rising from an original price of $125, its value on the secondary market now often exceeds $5,000.

This was an artist at the peak of his powers. In "A Little Bit Cautious," a big black bear gives an agitated porcupine a wide berth; the painting is redolent of October, with its gleaming beech leaves and sharp light, while the massive bear carries its physical and visual weight easily, paw caught in midstride, curiosity mixing with wariness. Ned revisited transparent watercolor, his first medium, in a series of upland gamebird paintings. One of the best is "Timber Baron," also an autumn scene (the season was, as Ned often admitted, his favorite), in which a long-bearded wild turkey pauses under a sugar maple, the background of rock ledges and trees handled loosely and in contrast to the crisp, glossy plumage of the bird.

One of Ned's last major oils, "Waiting for Dusk," painted two years before his death, started with the kernel of an idea: to show two red foxes in a snow-covered landscape. Sketching pencil thumbnails on the backs of rejected prints (the heavy, acid-free paper was perfect for drawing, and he was frugal enough not to want to waste such good stock), Ned worked through a variety *(text continues on page 42)*

Red foxes were a favorite animal of Ned Smith's, and he spent many hours over the years watching and photographing them hunting, playing, or tending their pups. His easy familiarity with the subject is apparent in these sketches, in which he works through the theme for a painting of a pair of foxes, trying out different poses and settings for what would eventually become one of his finest paintings, "Waiting for Dusk."

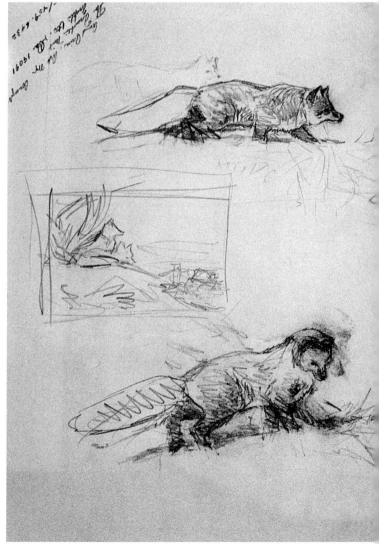

WAITING FOR DUSK
oil 1983 36 x 24 inches

of scenes and poses. In one, a fox trots jauntily along a stone wall; in another, one fox pounces on prey in a clump of grass while its mate watches nearby; in yet another, less developed sketch, a fox stalks something, its belly dragging through the snow.

Small as the thumbnails may be, they have an undeniable grace, especially those in which a fox is shown with its head bowed and neck curved, a posture that obviously attracted the artist increasingly as he worked through the concept. But among the several dozen roughs that cover three large sheets, there is one small, hastily sketched scene, little more than suggestive squiggles, that finally, to Ned's eye, hit the mark: two foxes sitting on a hill.

The painting that grew from that tiny germ perhaps illustrates the conjunction between place, subject, and the artist's lifetime of observation better than any work of Smith's. It is late afternoon on a winter day, with heavy snow lying on the ground. A pair of foxes waits on a pile of lichen-splashed sandstone—one sitting up, alert, watching the farmhouse and old barn in the hollow below, the other curled catlike on the rock, licking its chest, its neck curved in the smooth line that Smith had played with so often in his preliminary sketches. There is a rich, lingering light on the hills, which are unmistakably the Appalachians of central Pennsylvania. The red tinge to the mountains may be the sunset,

(text continues on page 47)

FLORIDA KEYS (2)
watercolor undated 18 x 15 inches

Although he often sketched scenes for future
reference, straight landscape painting wasn't
something Ned did with any great frequency.
The pair of early watercolors from the Florida
Keys were a gift to his wife after a vacation
there, while the moose hunters came out of one
of his trips to Canada.

MOOSE HUNTERS
watercolor undated 9 x 12 inches

One of two unfinished paintings on Smith's easels at the time of his death, this large oil of a herd of elk in the Canadian Rockies was a result of a recent trip the artist had made to the area.

UNTITLED
oil 1985 36 x 24 inches

© NED SMITH
1981

or it may be the first hint of spring, which makes the branches of the red maples flush crimson even in the snows of late winter. There is also a timeless quality to the scene, which speaks to season but not to year; there is an outhouse behind the main farmhouse, yet whether this is a glimpse of an earlier decade, or simply a crumbling, abandoned farm in current days, is left unclear.

In 1970, Ned Smith underwent open-heart surgery to replace a defective valve; he considered the years thereafter, which were his pinnacle professionally, to be a gift. Yet despite his heart problems, he did not slow down—he continued to fish and hike and canoe, to tote heavy camera equipment through the woods and drag whitetails down from the ridge tops each December during deer season, to stomp the hills on sweaty August days when little moved except the cicadas. He and Marie continued to travel to the Southwest, the Everglades, and the Canadian Rockies, where he sketched bighorn sheep and mountain goats, elk and mule deer, and painted landscape studies of the jagged peaks that would form the basis of new paintings.

In the early spring of 1985, he had two such western works well under way—an ambitious oil of a herd of bighorns in the high country, still with much of its underpainting exposed, and another, nearly finished, of a herd of elk in a mountain meadow. This was, he told friends, the direction in which he would increasingly move, but he'd also been busy in the preceding months with what for him were more typical subjects—prints of wild turkeys, brook trout, and other eastern species.

On April 22, 1985, Ned was working in the yard outside the home in Millersburg he'd shared with Marie for years, and which had grown into a thickly planted wildlife haven. Marie heard him call and knew from his voice something was wrong even before she ran out the door; he'd had a heart attack, and he was gone before the ambulance crew arrived.

News of Ned Smith's death shocked the conservation and art communities far beyond Pennsylvania, prompting an outpouring of tributes and memorials. But the test of any artist, of course, is time. Now, nearly two decades after his death, the enduring quality of his art and writing is clear, and their capacity to evoke place and emotion is just as strong. Just as Ned believed good paintings made him feel as though he'd been to the places he created, so much more powerfully do they transport us, too.

In "December Snow," the flakes drift down at a gentle slant, gathering in the corrugations in the bark of a fallen white pine. A big whitetail buck, bedded down beside the log, is watchful but not nervous, wrapped in the safety of the storm. There is a gauziness to the scene, a chill that comes not only through the cool greens and blue-grays of the painting's palette, but from the droop of the icy pine needles and the soft lines of the background—all in contrast to the high, sharp rack of the buck, which is echoed in the symmetrical branches of the dead tree and the twigs laced with newly fallen snow.

But within the artistic dazzle, at the painting's heart, there is—as in all of Ned Smith's works—a living, breathing animal, with snow melting beneath its warm body and catching on its eyelashes, and with a damp northeast wind playing around its ears. This is a single place, and a single time, but it is also universal. Look at the painting long enough and your own nose pinches with remembered cold.

DECEMBER SNOW
acrylic 1982 13 x 20 inches

The Art

Upland Gamebirds

As an illustrator whose clients frequently were sporting magazines and state wildlife agencies, it's no surprise that Ned Smith often painted gamebirds and other game animals—but they were also subjects with a lot of personal importance to him, since he was a lifelong hunter as well as a naturalist. That double familiarity brings an extra layer of meaning to Smith's game animal work, and a flair and intensity few other artists have captured.

In "Timber Baron," the setting is the mountainous, big-woods country of northern Pennsylvania, on an autumn day when the sugar maples and oaks have reached their peak of color. When Smith began his art career, wild turkeys were scarce in Pennsylvania, largely restricted to the remote Allegheny Plateau. Today they are common in the East, appearing in suburban neighborhoods and farmland woodlots, but Smith's turkey paintings often conveyed a lingering sense of the wilderness character this largest of upland gamebirds once represented.

TIMBER BARON (with preliminary sketches)
watercolor 1980 21 x 15 inches

If there was one subject that Smith returned to over the years with particular fondness, it was the ruffed grouse, which he considered the premier upland game-bird, as well as an endlessly fascinating object to draw and paint, with its complex plumage, majestic bearing, and riveting courtship display. In the display, the male mounts a fallen log, tail fanned and crest raised, and "drums" the air with its wings, creating a series of sharp booms that sputter slowly, accelerate to a rumble, and then die off, like a balky engine catching and then failing.

Over the decades, Smith spent countless spring dawns crouched in camouflaged blinds in the woods, hoping to get photographs of drumming males. The results were often spectacular, but not always. In the late 1960s, he spent months trying to photograph one cagey old male who drummed at dusk; he rigged his remote-controlled flash and telephoto lens during the afternoon while the bird was away from the drumming log.

About half an hour before dark a grouse began drumming *behind* the blind—possibly a hundred feet away. Grumbling at my bad luck, I sat it out anyhow, and it's a good thing I did. Eventually the drumming stopped, and before long I heard a grouse approaching. Barely discernible in the fading light he passed within a few feet of the blind, mounted the log, and immediately started drumming. Thankful that I had pre-focused the camera before dark, I snapped picture after picture while he continued beating out his challenge, unmindful of the blinding flash. When at length he fluttered up into a nearby tree to roost, I gathered my equipment and groped my way back to the car.

The transparencies arrived in today's mail from the processor, and they would be perfect except for one thing. The confounded bird had moulted every feather on top of his head, including, of course, the cocky crest that gives a grouse that aristocratic look. I now have a dozen pictures to prove that a bald-headed grouse is not a particularly handsome bird.

Never was Smith's mastery of grouse on better display than in "Windfall Grouse." In it, the male bird rockets out of a tangle of fallen white pine trunks and into the kind of second-growth jungle that grouse love, and through which grouse hunters are often forced to crash, branches lashing their faces raw. Smith chose an exceptionally tricky angle for the painting, a three-quarter view that flattens the bird's trademark fanned tail but still manages to preserve its subtle curves and shadows. Only someone who knew how grouse move, and how they're built, would attempt such a rough task, much less pull it off as handily as Smith did.

WINDFALL GROUSE
acrylic 1981 15 x 21 inches

THUNDER KING (with preliminary sketch)
watercolor 1980 21 x 15 inches

DEEP WOODS DRUMMER
watercolor 1970 12½ x 18 inches

DIXIE PRINCE
watercolor 1982 21 x 15 inches

*Spanish moss and an old sharecropper's cabin mark "Dixie Prince," a
late work of a flock of bobwhite, as quintessentially Southern,
hearkening back to Smith's early days working on the Samworth
plantation in South Carolina. "Windfall Woodcock" is a companion
piece to "Windfall Grouse."*

WINDFALL WOODCOCK
acrylic 1982 15 x 21 inches

EMPEROR OF CHINA
watercolor 1981 21 x 15 inches

*As with "Thunder King," "Dixie Prince," and "Timber
Baron," this watercolor was produced as part of a four-
plate print series featuring upland gamebirds.*

ROYAL DOMAIN
acrylic 1985 18 x 13 inches

DOGWOOD TIME GROUSE
watercolor 1984 23 x 15 inches

SPRINGTIME GROUSE
watercolor undated 21½ x 16 inches

RUFFED GROUSE
watercolor c. 1940 6¾ x 10 inches

NORTHERN BOBWHITE
watercolor c. 1940 6¾ x 10 inches

Two early watercolors show an emerging artist still well before his prime. They have a beginner's typically tentative use of color and mass, the lighting is flat, the vegetation is somewhat stylized, and Ned was obviously struggling with the overall design—but he was already an experienced bird hunter who knew that in the fall, ruffed grouse love wild fox grapes.

Waterfowl
and Water Birds

To the casual observer the high and dry portions of the cornfield seemed devoid of ducks, but the spotting scope revealed hundreds of blacks, mallards, and pintails feeding beneath the screen of broken cornstalks and rank weeds. All morning more pintails were arriving in small groups, racing in wide circles above the scene before setting their wings, arching their necks prettily, and gliding in to a masterful landing. He who first called them 'grey-hounds of the air' certainly knew waterfowl, for no other duck combines the pintail's sleek lines and dashing flight with his buoyant grace afloat."

—*Gone for the Day*

DROPPING IN
watercolor 1975 25 x 20 inches

AMERICAN WIGEON
acrylic 1981 15 x 33 inches

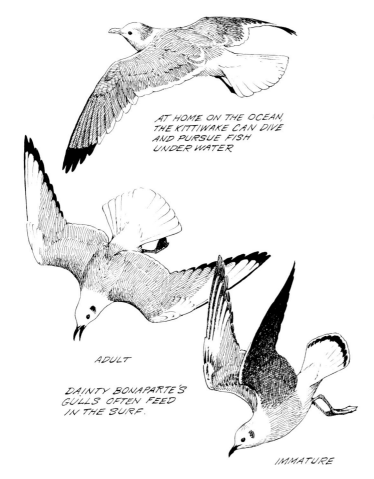

AT HOME ON THE OCEAN,
THE KITTIWAKE CAN DIVE
AND PURSUE FISH
UNDER WATER

ADULT

DAINTY BONAPARTE'S
GULLS OFTEN FEED
IN THE SURF.

IMMATURE

"Gannets wheel on immense outstretched wings just beyond the breakers. Scoters, eiders, and huge flocks of oldsquaws move closer to shore, and cormorants trade up and down the coastline in the troughs between the waves. Sprightly Bonaparte's gulls appear everywhere. When the east wind dies, the birds may be gone, but the watcher will hold the memory. He is convinced, despite red nose and watery eyes, that winter is the choice time to visit the sandy edge of the sea."
—Ned Smith's Wildlife Sketchbook

A GREAT BLACK-BACKED GULL PATROLS
THE BEACH WHILE A RUDDY TURNSTONE FLIPS
A SHELL IN ITS SEARCH FOR FOOD.

BEACH STROLLERS OFTEN ENCOUNTER WHELK EGG
CASES (ABOVE LEFT) AND HORSESHOE CRAB
SHELLS (ABOVE RIGHT) CAST UP BY WAVES.

WINTER BEACH
ink undated 14 x 8¼ inches

Living all his life along the Susquehanna River, one of the East's major flyways for migrating waterfowl, it's no wonder Ned Smith had an affinity for ducks, geese, and other water birds. He was an especially avid waterfowl hunter, and "Mallard Morning" is a scene he saw often each fall—a black Lab splashing out to make a retrieve while flocks of ducks trade back and forth overhead.

MALLARD MORNING
oil 1983 36 x 24 inches

GREATER SCAUP
acrylic undated 7 x 5 inches

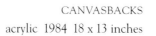

CANVASBACKS
acrylic 1984 18 x 13 inches

SNOWY EGRET
acrylic undated 12 x 8 inches

GREAT BLUE HERON
acrylic 1981 9¾ x 15⅛ inches

© NED SMITH
1981

Trout

THE INSPECTOR
mixed media undated 19½ x 11 inches

In the glassy tailwater of a long, slick pool, a brown trout rises to check out a mayfly before feeding—a situation Smith, a skilled fly-fisherman, knew well. "The Inspector" is a mixed media work he did for his friend, the noted fishing writer Sam Slaymaker.

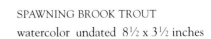

SPAWNING BROOK TROUT
watercolor undated 8½ x 3½ inches

THE LAST DRAKE
acrylic 1984 18 x 13 inches

*The green drake—the largest mayfly on many Pennsylvania
streams, which emerges in early summer just when the
mountain laurel is blooming—brings even the biggest, wariest
trout to the surface, like the lunker brook trout in this
painting, which was the 1985 conservation stamp print for the
Pennsylvania Federation of Sportsmen's Clubs.*

BROOK TROUT
pencil undated 13 x 5 inches

"*About two o'clock I wandered into a real picturebook spot along the creek—a deep, clear pool backed by a sheer, rocky, moss-carpeted cliff. A single redbud tree grew from a toehold among the boulders and the smooth water mirrored its delicate beauty. Then, to make things incredibly perfect, a nice trout rose in the middle of the reflection to suck in a drifting Mayfly, and I suddenly remembered the flyrod in my hand.*"—Gone for the Day

Songbirds and Raptors

WINTER FEEDER BIRDS
acrylic undated
32 x 25 inches

This scene of evening grosbeaks, purple finches, blue jays, and other common winter birds looks a great deal like the scene just outside Ned Smith's sliding glass studio door, in Ned and Marie's heavily landscaped yard.

EASTERN MEADOWLARK
acrylic 1978 10⅛ x 15 inches

These field studies of thrushes, horned larks, and warblers manage, in an economy of lines and watercolor washes, to capture the attitudes and personalities of the birds, which were drawn from life. Although Smith used his camera extensively to document animals and their habitats, field observation and sketching were central to his art.

CAUGHT NAPPING
acrylic 1983 16 x 20 inches

In the early 1980s, birders across the East were electrified to discover that a pair of gyrfalcons—the largest falcons in the world—had come down from the Arctic to winter in the Amish farmland of Pennsylvania. "Caught Napping" shows the almost black female with a goldeneye she's killed amid the ice floes of the Susquehanna River.

KEEPER OF THE CLIFFS
acrylic 1984 17 x 23½ inches

PEREGRINE FALCON
acrylic 1978 16 x 24 inches

When Ned Smith did this cover (left) and an accompanying article for
Pennsylvania Game News, *the peregrine falcon's fortunes had begun the most*
tentative of recoveries. When Smith was growing up, the "duck hawk" had nested
on cliffs along the Susquehanna and Juniata rivers, but DDT contamination had
wiped them out as a breeding species in the East by the 1960s. In the 1970s, the
Peregrine Fund reintroduced captive-bred falcons to the wild in Pennsylvania and
surrounding states, an arduous and expensive project that eventually returned the
birds to many of their former haunts. But while peregrines now nest on bridges and
buildings in several urban areas in Pennsylvania, they have only just begun to
reclaim their traditional cliff eyries along the Susquehanna (like the one he
depicted) perhaps kept away by predation from great horned owls.

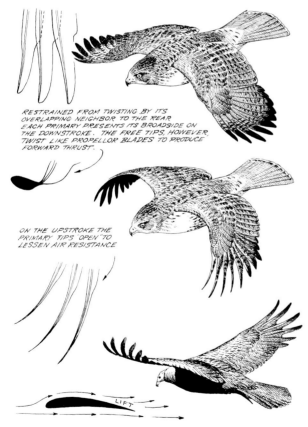

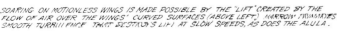

A red-tailed hawk and turkey vulture illustrate how
birds' wings generate lift in this ink drawing from
the "Wildlife Sketchbook" column.

COURTESY NATIONAL WILDLIFE FEDERATION

CEDAR WAXWINGS
watercolor and pencil undated
13 x 9½ inches

CAVITY-NESTING BIRDS
acrylic undated 21 x 26 inches

*Painted to illustrate an article
on cavity-nesting birds,
this montage groups eastern
bluebird, the endangered
spotted owl and red-cockaded
woodpecker, wood duck,
prothonotary warbler, and
pileated woodpecker.*

BROADWING FLIGHT
acrylic 1982
13 x 20 inches

"September 22—My bird-watching crony and I journeyed to Hawk Mountain this morning, hoping to catch a good flight of broad-winged hawks . . . about ten o'clock the first hawks appeared over the far ridge—tiny black pinpoints that slowly materialized into broadwings. They were high, gliding erratically, now coming straight-on, now circling over one spot. Soon others came into view, a dozen at a time; still later, flocks of thirty to fifty. By noon we were almost too busy counting to eat. All afternoon they streamed by, and when the last hawk disappeared into the distance the tally stood at 2,811. So completely had broadwings preempted the stage that only five other hawks showed up—one each redtail, sharpshin, marsh hawk, peregrine (a rather rare one), and osprey." —Gone for the Day

Big Game and Other Mammals

When Ned graduated from high school, he and a friend
took a canoe trip through the lake country of eastern
Canada, during which he saw his first wild moose.
"Testing the Wind," which came late in the artist's career,
drew on this and many return trips to the region, with its
cold bogs and dark spruce forests.

TESTING THE WIND
oil 1983 36 x 24 inches

IDAHO BULL
acrylic undated 27 x 18¾ inches

Painted in the early 1970s, "Idaho Bull" catches an elk hunt at a pivotal moment—the mounted hunter is leaping from his horse as the big bull, muscles bunched, leaps for heavy cover and safety. Originally painted as a commission for a natural history museum, which subsequently rejected it because of the inclusion of the hunter, the acrylic was acquired by a private buyer and is now in the collection of the Ned Smith Center for Nature and Art.

whitetail preliminary sketch
pencil undated 12 x 14 inches

In Pennsylvania, antlered deer season traditionally opens the Monday following Thanksgiving, a day when rural school districts and businesses still often close because so many people are in the woods.

> "Opening day for bucks, and I thought it would never arrive! . . . There's nothing so suspenseful as those last few minutes before the magic opening hour on opening day. You scarcely breathe, straining to catch the first sound or glimpse of a moving deer. Each faint rustle is analyzed, each flicker of movement scrutinized. Nothing is taken for granted." —Gone for the Day

Some of that mystery and suspense comes through in "Moonlight Buck." One of Ned's more unusual deer paintings, it employs a limited palette of blues and grays to convey a frosty full-moon night in the depths of winter. The long shadows accentuate the painting's somewhat expanded horizontal format, which lends tension to the otherwise quiet scene. Interestingly, the buck—although respectable in any hunter's eye—doesn't sport a monstrous rack. Ned rarely exaggerated the antlers of the deer he drew, preferring to show the kind of whitetails most people encountered in the wild.

MOONLIGHT BUCK
acrylic 1970 18¾ x 11 inches

If grouse were Ned Smith's favorite subject, white-tailed
deer ran a close second, and he probably drew and painted
more of them than anything else. "Old Orchard Buck" is a
late oil, painted specifically for the fine-art print market.
It's possible that no artist painted white-tailed deer as well
as Smith, who had an uncanny ability, regardless of the
media, to capture the grace, power, and intelligence of this
quintessential big game animal.

thumbnail sketches: deer, bear, turkey
pencil undated 18½ x 25½ inches

OLD ORCHARD BUCK
oil 1983 36 x 24 inches

AFTER THE STORM
acrylic 1984 18½ x 23½ inches

BIG RED
acrylic 1978 17 x 24¾ inches

"The advent of winter calls for a change of clothing for wildlife as well as for humans . . . The snowshoe hare not only turns white in winter, but its huge feet are made even bigger by a fringe of stiff hairs that creates wonderfully effective snowshoes." —Ned Smith's Wildlife Sketchbook

BIGHORN HERO (unfinished)
oil 1985 36 x 24 inches

Uncompleted at the time of the artist's death, this painting grew out of his travels in the Canadian Rockies, which produced the field sketch (left) of Banff National Park and a series of preliminary pencil drawings like the one at top left. Large areas of underpainting are visible in the sky and boulders, and in the roughly sketched bighorns to the rear of the herd; even the lead ram, while more fully rendered, is in a preliminary state.

"Often, a wolf pack will sneak as close as possible to its prey without being detected, then once discovered, will quickly close the gap. Should the moose stand its ground, the wolves will usually go on their way. But if it takes to its heels, the chase will soon be on."
—Ned Smith's Wildlife Sketchbook

CLOSING IN
oil 1982 23 x 15 inches

© Ned Smith
1982

RED FOX
ink undated 9 x 7 inches

"Unlike their gray cousins, red foxes do not like being underground. They will
usually run before hounds all day and all night rather than hole up. They even
prefer curling up on the snow to napping underground."
                                        —Ned Smith's Wildlife Sketchbook

"If there's a time in each year when all wildlife is in the pink of condition, it is
October . . . To my mind, at least, the personification of vigorous good health
is the white-tailed buck. He is at his heaviest now, hard of muscle and well
larded, too—the result of an abundance of mast and browse. His thin red
summer hair has been replaced by a dense, glossy coat of gray-brown. His
antlers, rubbed free of the last traces of velvet, glisten in the sun as he tosses up
his head to catch a distant sound." —Gone for the Day

BIRCH BOTTOM BUCK
acrylic 1982 11 x 17 inches

Pencil and Line Art

Ned Smith's most supple and graceful illustrations were often those in black and white, in which he could focus on form and contrast without worrying about color. He refined his chiaroscuro technique in the 1950s doing magazine illustrations, working on a toned illustration board with a mix of dark pencil and white tempera for highlights, and produced some of his best work in this medium in the '60s and '70s. The leaping buck (right) appeared in his "Gone for the Day" column in December 1967.

To produce ink drawings like the racoon and white-tailed deer on page 101, Smith relied on a crow-quill pen and ink bottle rather than mechanical drawing pens. While the steel-nibbed crow-quill pen was balky and difficult to control, he felt it gave him crisper results and better control of line density.

LEAPING BUCK
pencil and white tempera 1967 9¼ x 14 inches

RACCOON
ink 1979 9½ x 7½ inches

WHITE-TAILED BUCK
ink 1979 10½ x 10 inches

From the barely mobile sloth to the swift cheetah (with a human runner well back in the pack), the relative running speeds of a number of mammals are shown in this two-panel drawing done for National Geographic's two-volume Book of Mammals.

COURTESY NATIONAL GEOGRAPHIC SOCIETY

A spotted skunk assumes a defensive posture.

COURTESY NATIONAL GEOGRAPHIC SOCIETY

RUNNING MAMMALS
ink 1981 16 x 9 inches each

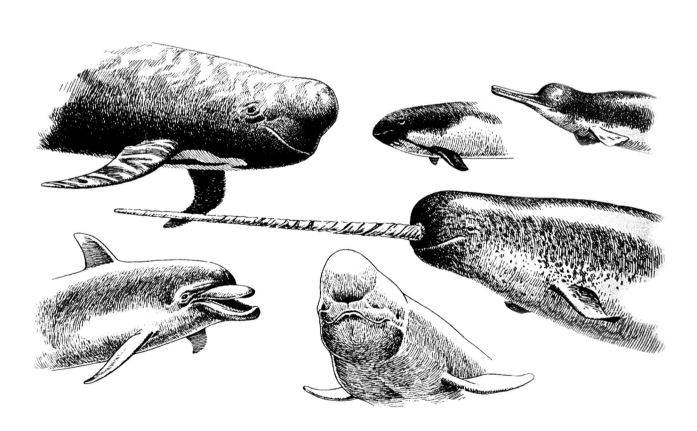

*This group portrait of six different cetaceans
was done for the National Geographic Society.*

COURTESY NATIONAL GEOGRAPHIC SOCIETY

One of Smith's abiding passions was prehistoric archaeology, sparked at an early age by hunting for projectile points and potsherds in freshly plowed fields along the Susquehanna River, once a major trade corridor for the Susquehannock, Lenape, Shawnee, Iroquois, and other tribes. He never lost his enthusiasm for the subject, or for looking for evidence of past eras of history, as he described in *Gone for the Day*:

May 3—After looking over a friend's plowed field several times this spring we made one last inspection, and I'm glad we did. Marie was most successful. Her first find was a small but extremely well-made flint spear point with skillfully formed corner notches. A second, but larger, black spear point was beautifully flaked but the base was slightly damaged. The third point was a rather crude spear point—like the second, a late Archaic projectile possibly three or four thousand years old. My only find was a triangular arrowhead. Archaeological evidence supports the theory that the bow and arrow were not used in what is now Pennsylvania until a few hundred years B.C., and that the triangular point, without notches or shank, was the only form of arrow point used here. The other types are chiefly spear or javelin points—even the very small notched types.

ABOVE – JAVELIN POINTS

BELOW – ARROWHEADS

As he matured, Ned's interest turned from simply collecting artifacts (a common hobby in this archaeologically rich area) to a more methodical approach to the subject. He sometimes worked side-by-side with archaeologists from the state museum and used the same careful techniques on his own excavations.

In the late 1960s, for example, Ned and his friends Jack Miller and Jim Hoy, who owned an island on the river, noticed that a storm had brought down several trees there—and that among the torn-up roots were a number of stone artifacts. Ned knew the islands had been used for millennia as fishing camps and way-stations, but the number of stone points and pieces of pottery made him wonder if a more permanent dwelling hadn't been built there—a structure whose old post-holes and hearths might still be preserved underground. He measured out five-foot squares over the site and began a meticulous excavation, documenting what he found through notes, drawings, and photographs—a process that even he admitted was "tedious and back-breaking." Marie, who helped on many such digs, later recalled (somewhat ruefully) that they rarely came home before dark. "You haven't lived until you've gone five feet down with a trowel," she remembered. "Ned wouldn't do it any other way. He was so scientific."

Although they found hearths, with their characteristically oxidized soil from the heat of the fire, Ned and Marie were unable to find evidence of the dwelling he suspected was there. Nor was that the only such excavation he undertook—when floods from tropical storm Agnes in 1972 stripped vegetation off another island, exposing a camp, he and Marie scrambled to document it before the freshly revealed objects eroded away, and he prospected for evidence of human habitation in local rock shelters and stream valleys.

In 1975, Ned traveled to southwestern Pennsylvania to write and illustrate an article on the Meadowcroft Rock Shelter, an important Paleolithic site that literally rewrote the history of humans in the New World. Evidence of human occupation at Meadowcroft has been documented as far back as at least sixteen thousand years, making it the oldest well-dated archaeological site in North America. Ned's pencil illustrations depicted later Woodland Indian inhabitants at the shelter.

MEADOWCROFT ROCK SHELTER
pencil 1975 10 x 13 inches

A unique sequence done against a black background shows a tropical fishing bat nabbing its prey.

Three ink drawings portray birds common to central Pennsylvania: a turkey vulture, a male and female rufous-sided towhee (now eastern towhee), and a northern flicker, feeding on the ground.

RUFOUS-SIDED TOWHEES
ink 1979 7½ x 9½ inches

GREAT HORNBILL
pencil 1975 10½ x 15 inches

The great hornbill, which walls up its chicks inside a hollow tree and feeds them through a hole until they fledge, is an Asian species.

COURTESY NATIONAL WILDLIFE FEDERATION

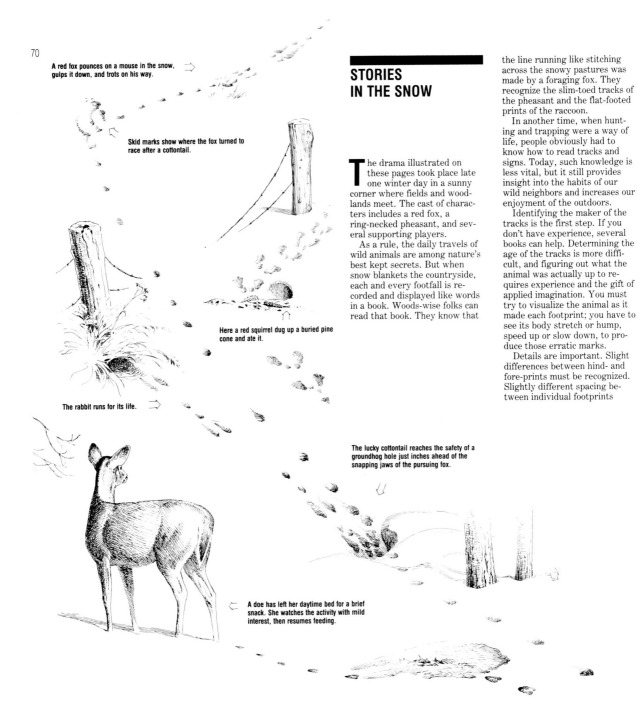

70

A red fox pounces on a mouse in the snow, gulps it down, and trots on his way.

Skid marks show where the fox turned to race after a cottontail.

Here a red squirrel dug up a buried pine cone and ate it.

The rabbit runs for its life.

The lucky cottontail reaches the safety of a groundhog hole just inches ahead of the snapping jaws of the pursuing fox.

A doe has left her daytime bed for a brief snack. She watches the activity with mild interest, then resumes feeding.

STORIES IN THE SNOW

The drama illustrated on these pages took place late one winter day in a sunny corner where fields and woodlands meet. The cast of characters includes a red fox, a ring-necked pheasant, and several supporting players.

As a rule, the daily travels of wild animals are among nature's best kept secrets. But when snow blankets the countryside, each and every footfall is recorded and displayed like words in a book. Woods-wise folks can read that book. They know that the line running like stitching across the snowy pastures was made by a foraging fox. They recognize the slim-toed tracks of the pheasant and the flat-footed prints of the raccoon.

In another time, when hunting and trapping were a way of life, people obviously had to know how to read tracks and signs. Today, such knowledge is less vital, but it still provides insight into the habits of our wild neighbors and increases our enjoyment of the outdoors.

Identifying the maker of the tracks is the first step. If you don't have experience, several books can help. Determining the age of the tracks is more difficult, and figuring out what the animal was actually up to requires experience and the gift of applied imagination. You must try to visualize the animal as it made each footprint; you have to see its body stretch or hump, speed up or slow down, to produce those erratic marks.

Details are important. Slight differences between hind- and fore-prints must be recognized. Slightly different spacing between individual footprints

This two-panel illustration, drawn for the "Wildlife Sketchbook" column in National Wildlife, *is a masterwork of simplicity and composition—and also reflects Smith's long fascination with tracks and trails, which he photographed and sketched obsessively.* COURTESY NATIONAL WILDLIFE FEDERATION

should be noted; they mean a change in speed. Gradually, the picture takes shape, like a movie composed of split second frames, until finally the creature's actions are reconstructed from the evidence in the snow.

A mile of fox meanderings has been compressed to fit these pages, cutting out some uneventful stretches and retaining a number of interesting diversions. Notice how each quick turn, crouch, sudden rush or twisting leap is signified by a break in the evenly spaced pattern of trotting footprints.

Note the gashes made by the birds' wingtips on takeoff and the tail feathers braking for a landing. Without the accompanying interpretation these could be difficult to decipher, but unless their meaning is discovered there is little excitement in following the trails.

Track reading can be fun anywhere there is snow. In a north country spruce forest, the tracks of moose, wolves, fishers,

snowshoe hares and spruce grouse might be encountered. Rocky Mountain foothills might be laced with the trails of elk, pronghorns, jackrabbits, coyotes and magpies. Even suburban areas reveal a surprising number of inhabitants, ranging from dogs and cats to pheasants, raccoons, and opossums.

The roll call of inhabitants, of course, is only the beginning. Uncounted adventures are recorded across the face of each pristine field and woodland. But for every line that is read, a thousand chapters will be erased by the next snowfall.

A cock pheasant, flushed by a snooping dog, lands in a nearby field, its long tail feathers tracing a pretty design in the snow.

Sensing no danger, the cock moves on, feeding on waste corn as it goes.

Here the cock stopped to enjoy the warm sunshine in the shelter of some brambles.

A crow takes wing and follows the fox, taunting it with loud, snarling caws.

Getting wind of the pheasant, the fox sneaks closer, then leaps. But the pheasant, alerted by the crow's fussing, escapes the rush.

WINTER TRACKS
ink undated 17¼ x 20½ each

GRAY SQUIRREL
monochromatic watercolor undated 14½ x 9 inches

ACKNOWLEDGMENTS

THIS PROJECT WOULD NOT HAVE BEEN POSSIBLE WITHOUT THE ENTHUSI-astic support of the board and staff of the Ned Smith Center for Nature and Art, which made its large collection of original art available for reproduction. I am also indebted to Steve Burrik of Sportsman Special-ties, who was Ned Smith's print publisher; to Carl Graybill and Hal Kor-ber of the Pennsylvania Game Commission; and to Robert McNeill for allowing several important pieces in his private collection to be pho-tographed for this book. Thanks as well to Karl Blankenship and Kath-leen Gaskell for providing oral history interviews, and to Sylvia Bashline for permission to draw on material written by her late husband, Jim Bash-line, who was Ned's friend and editor. The Academy of Natural Sciences in Philadelphia gave permission for the use of excerpts from Ned Smith's unpublished journals, while the National Geographic Society and National Wildlife Federation allowed the reproduction of illustrations.

Finally, thanks to Stackpole Books editor Mark Allison for undertak-ing this project, and to my late friend Marie Smith for ensuring that Ned's work will continue to inspire generations to come.

BIRDERS
ink undated 8½ x 11 inches
COURTESY NATIONAL WILDLIFE FEDERATION

*"To anyone else, a bird watcher is something of a kook. But instead of selling them
short, I've got a better idea . . . put yourself in the hands of your neighborhood bird-
watcher for a day during the May migrations. If you aren't surprised at the beauty of
our birds close up, if you aren't amazed by their variety, if you don't find that a
knowledge of birds adds interest to your days afield, if you don't have a darned good
time—you may write me a nasty letter to that effect. I probably won't answer it, but
I assure you I'll read it—and I'll put you on my private kook list."*

—Gone for the Day

RING-NECKED PHEASANT
watercolor 1982 15 x 17 inches

This unusual piece, one of a pair painted on a black background to accentuate the theme of impending extinction, was commissioned by the National Wildlife Federation for a publication on endangered species. It includes a whooping crane, American crocodile, blue pike, Florida atala butterfly, gray wolf, and trailing arbutus.

ENDANGERED SPECIES
gouache undated 21 x 14 inches

INDEX OF ARTWORK